The

London Baptist Confession

of Faith

1677-89

By

Various

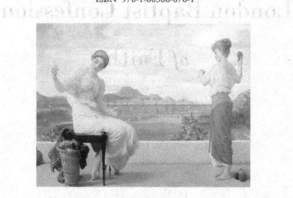

The 1677-89 London Baptist Confession *of* Faith

Thirty-Two Articles *of*
Christian Faith *and* Practice

Adopted *by the*
Ministers *and* Messengers
of the General Assembly
Which Met *in* London *in* 1689

Contents

Contents

To *the* Judicious
and Impartial Reader

Courteous Reader,

I t is now many years since many of us (with other sober Christians then living and walking in the way of the Lord that we profess) did conceive ourselves to be under a necessity of Publishing a Confession of our Faith, for the information, and satisfaction of those, that did not thoroughly understand what our principles were, or had entertained prejudices against our Profession, by reason of the strange representation of them, by some men of note, who had taken very wrong measures, and accordingly led others into misapprehensions, of us, and them: and this was first put forth about the year, 1643. in the name of seven Congregations then gathered in London; since which time, diverse impressions thereof have been dispersed abroad, and our end proposed, in good measure answered, inasmuch as many (and some of those men eminent, both for piety and learning) were thereby satisfied, that we were no way guilty of those Heterodoxies and fundamental errors, which had too frequently been charged upon us without ground, or occasion given on our part. And forasmuch, as that Confession is not now commonly to be had; and also that many others have since embraced the same truth which is owned therein; it was judged necessary by us to join together in giving a testimony to the world; of our firm adhering to those wholesome Principles, by the publication of this which is now in your hand.

And forasmuch as our method, and manner of expressing our sentiments, in this, doth vary from the former (although the substance of the matter is the same) we shall freely impart to you the reason and occasion thereof. One thing that greatly prevailed with us to undertake this work, was (not only to give a full account of our selves, to those Christians that differ from us about the subject of Baptism, but also) the profit that might from thence arise, unto those that have any account of our labors, in their instruction, and establishment in the great truths of the Gospel; in the clear understanding, and steady belief of which, our comfortable walking with God, and fruitfulness before him, in all our ways, is most nearly concerned; and therefore we did conclude it necessary to express our selves the more fully, and distinctly; and also to fix on such a method as might be most comprehensive of those things which we designed to explain our sense, and belief of; and finding no defect, in this regard, in that fixed on by the assembly, and after them by those of the Congregational way, we did readily conclude it best to retain the same order in our present confession: and also, when we observed that those last mentioned, did in their confession (for reasons which seemed of weight both to themselves and others) choose not only to express their mind in words concurrent with the former in sense, concerning all those articles wherein they were agreed, but also for the most part without any variation of the terms we did in like manner conclude it best to follow their example in making use of the very same words with them both, in these articles (which are very many) wherein our faith and doctrine is the same with theirs, and this we did, the more abundantly, to manifest our consent with both, in all the fundamental articles of the Christian Religion, as also with many others, whose orthodox confessions have been published to the world; on behalf of the Protestants in divers Nations and Cities: and also to convince all, that we have no itch to clog Religion with new words, but do readily acquiesce in that form of sound words, which hath been, in consent with the holy Scriptures, used by others before us; hereby declaring before God, Angels, & Men, our hearty agreement with them, in that wholesome Protestant Doctrine, which with so clear evidence of Scriptures they have asserted: some things indeed, are in some places added, some terms omitted, and some few changed, but these alterations are of that nature, as that we need not doubt, any charge or suspicion of unsoundness in the faith, from any of our brethren upon the account of them.

In those things wherein we differ from others, we have expressed ourselves with all candor and plainness that none might entertain jealousy of ought secretly lodged in our breasts, that we would not the world should be acquainted with; yet we hope we have also observed those rules of modesty, and humility, as will render our freedom in this respect inoffensive, even to those whose sentiments are different from ours.

We have also taken care to affix texts of Scripture, in the margin for the confirmation of each article in our confession; in which work we have studiously endeavored to select such as are most clear and pertinent, for the proof of what is asserted by us: and our earnest desire is, that all into whose hands this may come, would follow that (never enough commended) example of the noble Bereans,[1] who searched the Scriptures daily, that they might find out whether the things preached to them were so or not.

There is one thing more which we sincerely profess, and earnestly desire credence in, *viz.* That contention is most remote from our design in all that we have done in this matter: and we hope the liberty of an ingenuous unfolding our principles, and opening our hearts unto our Brethren, with the Scripture grounds on which our faith and practice leans, will by none of them be either denied to us, or taken ill from us. Our whole design is accomplished, if we may obtain that Justice, as to be measured in our principles, and practice, and the judgment of both by others, according to what we have now published; which the Lord (whose eyes are as a flame of fire) knoweth to be the doctrine, which with our hearts we must firmly believe, and sincerely endeavor to conform our lives to. And oh that other contentions being laid asleep, the only care and contention of all upon whom the name of our blessed Redeemer is called, might for the future be, to walk humbly with their God, and in the exercise of all Love and Meekness towards each other, to perfect holiness in the fear of the Lord, each one endeavoring to have his conversation such as becometh the Gospel; and also suitable to his place and capacity vigorously to promote in others the practice of true Religion and undefiled in the sight of God and our Father. And that in this backsliding day, we might not spend our breath in

---

[1] *The inhabitants of the city of Berea, also known in the Bible as Beroea, and now known as Veria in what is today Greek Macedonia, northern Greece.*

fruitless complaints of the evils of others; but may every one begin at home, to reform in the first place our own hearts, and ways; and then to quicken all that we may have influence upon, to the same work; that if the will of God were so, none might deceive themselves, by resting in, and trusting to, a form of Godliness, without the power of it, and inward experience of the efficacy of those truths that are professed by them.

And verily there is one spring and cause of the decay of Religion in our day, which we cannot but touch upon, and earnestly urge a redress of; and that is the neglect of the worship of God in Families, by those to whom the charge and conduct of them is committed. May not the gross ignorance, and instability of many; with the profaneness of others, be justly charged upon their Parents and Masters; who have not trained them up in the way wherein they ought to walk when they were young? but have neglected those frequent and solemn commands which the Lord hath laid upon them so to catechize, and instruct them, that their tender years might be seasoned with the knowledge of the truth of God as revealed in the Scriptures; and also by their own omission of Prayer, and other duties of Religion in their families, together with the ill example of their loose conversation, have inured them first to a neglect, and then contempt of all Piety and Religion? we know this will not excuse the blindness, or wickedness of any; but certainly it will fall heavy upon those that have thus been the occasion thereof; they indeed dye in their sins; but will not their blood be required of those under whose care they were, who yet permitted them to go on without warning, yea led them into the paths of destruction? and will not the diligence of Christians with respect to the discharge of these duties, in ages past, rise up in judgment against, and condemn many of those who would be esteemed such now?

We shall conclude with our earnest prayer, that the God of all grace, will pour out those measures of his holy Spirit upon us, that the profession of truth may be accompanied with the sound belief, and diligent practice of it by us; that his name may in all things be glorified, through Jesus Christ our Lord, Amen.

Chapter I

Of *the* Holy Scriptures

1. The Holy Scripture is the only sufficient, certain, and infallible[2] rule of all saving Knowledge, Faith and Obedience; Although the[3] light of Nature, and the works of Creation and Providence do so far manifest the goodness, wisdom and power of God, as to leave men inexcusable; yet are they not sufficient to give that knowledge of God and His will, which is necessary unto Salvation.[4] Therefore it pleased the Lord at sundry times, and in divers manners, to reveal himself, and to declare that His will unto his Church; and afterward for the better preserving, and propagating of the Truth, and for the more sure Establishment, and Comfort of the Church against the corruption of the flesh, and the malice of Satan, and of the World, to commit the same wholly unto[5] writing; which maketh the Holy Scriptures to be most necessary, those former ways of Gods revealing his will unto his people being now ceased.

2. Under the Name of Holy Scripture or the written Word of God; are now contained all the Books of the Old and New Testament which are these,

Of *the* Old Testament

Genesis, Exodus, Leviticus, Numbers, Deuteronomy, Joshua, Judges, Ruth, 1 Samuel, 2 Samuel, 1 Kings, 2 Kings, 1 Chronicles, 2 Chronicles, Ezra, Nehemiah, Esther, Job, Psalms, Proverbs, Ecclesiastes, The Song of Songs, Isaiah, Jeremiah, Lamentations, Ezekiel, Daniel, Hosea, Joel, Amos, Obadiah, Jonah, Micah, Nahum, Habakkuk, Zephaniah, Haggai, Zechariah, Malachi.

---

[2] *2 Tim. 3. 15,16,17. Isa. 8. 20. Luk. 16. 29, 31. Eph. 2. 20.*
[3] *Rom. 1. 19, 20, 21. etc. ch 2. 14, 15. Psal. 19. 1, 2, 3.*
[4] *Heb. 1. 1.*
[5] *Pro. 22. 19, 20, 21. Rom. 15. 4. 2 Pet. 1. 19, 20.*

Of *the* New Testament

Matthew, Mark, Luke, John, The Acts of the Apostles, Pauls Epistle to the Romans, 1 Corinthians, 2 Corinthians, Galatians, Ephesians, Phillippians, Colossians, 1 Thessalonians, 2 Thessalonians, 1 Timothy, 2 Timothy, to Titus, to Philemon, the Epistle to the Hebrews, the Epistle of James, The first and second Epistles of Peter, The first, second and third Epistles of John, the Epistle of Jude, the Revelation.

All which are given by the[6] inspiration of God, to be the rule of Faith and Life.

3. The Books commonly called Apocrypha not being of[7] Divine inspiration, are no part of the Canon (or rule) of the Scripture, and therefore are of no authority to the Church of God, nor to be any otherwise approved or made use of, then other humane writings.

4. The Authority of the Holy Scripture for which it ought to be believed dependeth not upon the testimony of any man, or Church; but wholly upon[8] God (who is truth itself) the Author thereof; therefore it is to be received, because it is the Word of God.

5. We may be moved and induced by the testimony of the Church of God, to an high and reverent esteem of the Holy Scriptures; and the heavenliness of the matter, the efficacy of the Doctrine, and the Majesty of the stile, the consent of all the parts, the scope of the whole (which is to give all glory to God) the full discovery it makes of the only way of mans salvation, and many other incomparable Excellencies, and entire perfections thereof, are arguments whereby it doth abundantly evidence itself to be the Word of God; yet notwithstanding; our[9] full persuasion, and assurance of the infallible truth, and divine authority thereof, is from the inward work of the Holy Spirit, bearing witness by and with the Word in our Hearts.

---

[6] *2 Tim. 3. 16.*
[7] *Luk. 24. 27, 44. Rom. 3. 2.*
[8] *2 Pet. 1. 19, 20, 21. 2 Tim. 3. 16. 2 Thes. 2. 13. 1 Joh. 5. 9.*
[9] *Joh. 16. 13, 14. 1 Cor. 2. 10, 11, 12. 1 John 2. 2.20.27.*

6. The whole Council of God concerning all things[10] necessary for his own Glory, Mans Salvation, Faith and Life, is either expressly set down or necessarily contained in the Holy Scripture; unto which nothing at any time is to be added, whether by new Revelation of the Spirit, or traditions of men.

Nevertheless we acknowledge the[11] inward illumination of the Spirit of God, to be necessary for the saving understanding of such things as are revealed in the Word, and that there are some circumstances concerning the worship of God, and government of the Church common to humane actions and societies; which are to be[12] ordered by the light of nature, and Christian prudence according to the general rules of the Word, which are always to be observed.

7. All things in Scripture are not alike[13] plain in themselves, nor alike clear unto all; yet those things which are necessary to be known, believed, and observed for Salvation, are so[14] clearly propounded, and opened in some place of Scripture or other, that not only the learned, but the unlearned, in a due use of ordinary means, may attain to a sufficient understanding of them.

8. The Old Testament in[15] Hebrew, (which was the Native language of the people of God of old) and the New Testament in Greek (which at the time of the writing of it was most generally known to the Nations being immediately inspired by God, and by his singular care and Providence kept pure in all Ages, are therefore[16] authentical; so as in all controversies of Religion the Church is finally to appeal unto them[17] But because these original tongues are not known to all the people of God, who have a right unto, and interest in the Scriptures, and are commanded in the fear of God to read[18] and search them, therefore they are to be translated into the

---

[10] *2 Tim. 3. 15, 16, 17. Gal. 1. 8, 9.*
[11] *John 6. 45. 1 Cor. 2. 9, 10, 11, 12.*
[12] *1 Cor. 11, 13, 14. & ch. 14. 26. & 40.*
[13] *2 Pet. 3. 16.*
[14] *Ps. 19. 7. and 119. 130.*
[15] *Rom. 3. 2.*
[16] *Isa. 8. 20.*
[17] *Act. 15. 15.*
[18] *John 5. 39.*

vulgar language of every Nation, unto which they[19] come, that the Word of God dwelling[20] plentifully in all, they may worship Him in an acceptable manner, and through patience and comfort of the Scriptures may have hope.

9. The infallible rule of interpretation of Scripture is the[21] Scripture itself: And therefore when there is a question about the true and full sense of any Scripture (which is not manifold but one) it must be searched by other places that speak more clearly.

10. The supreme judge by which all controversies of Religion are to be determined, and all Decrees of Councils, opinions of ancient Writers, Doctrines of men, and private Spirits, are to be examined, and in whose sentence we are to rest, can be no other but the Holy Scripture delivered by the Spirit, into which[22] Scripture so delivered, our faith is finally resolved.

---

[19] 1 Cor. 14, 6.9.11,12.24.28.
[20] Col. 3. 16.
[21] 2 Pet. 1. 20, 21. Act. 15. 15, 16.
[22] Mat. 22. 29.31. Eph. 2. 20. Acts 28. 23.

Chapter II

Of God *and of the* Holy Trinity

1. The Lord our God is but[23] one only living, and true God; whose[24] subsistence is in and of himself,[25] infinite in being, and perfection, whose Essence cannot be comprehended by any but himself;[26] a most pure spirit,[27] invisible, without body, parts, or passions, who only hath immortality, dwelling in the light, which no man can approach unto, who is[28] immutable,[29] immense,[30] eternal, incomprehensible,[31] Almighty, every way infinite,[32] most holy, most wise, most free, most absolute,[33] working all things according to the council of his own immutable, and most righteous will,[34] for his own glory, most loving, gracious, merciful, long suffering, abundant in goodness and truth, forgiving iniquity, transgression and sin,[35] the rewarder of them that diligently seek him, and with all most just,[36] and terrible in his judgments,[37] hating all sin, and who will by no means clear the[38] guilty.

2. God having all[39] life,[40] glory,[41] goodness, blessedness, in and of himself: is alone in, and unto himself all-sufficient, not[42] standing in

---

[23] *1 Cor. 8.4 6. Deut. 6.4.*
[24] *Jer 10.10. Isaiah 48.12.*
[25] *Exod 3.14.*
[26] *Joh. 4.24.*
[27] *1 Tim. 1.17. Deut. 4.15,16.*
[28] *Mal. 3.6.*
[29] *1 King. 8.27. Jer. 23.23.*
[30] *Ps. 90.2.*
[31] *Gen. 17.1.*
[32] *Isa. 6.3.*
[33] *Ps. 115.3. Isa. 46.10.*
[34] *Pro. 16.4. Rom. 11.36.*
[35] *Exod. 34.6,7. Hebr. 11.6.*
[36] *Neh. 9.32,33.*
[37] *Ps. 5.5,6.*
[38] *Exod. 34.7. Nahum. 1,2,3.*
[39] *Joh. 5.26.*
[40] *Ps. 148.13.*
[41] *Ps. 119.68.*

need of any Creature which He hath made, nor deriving any glory from them, but only manifesting his own glory in, by, unto, and upon them, He is the alone fountain of all Being,[43] of whom, through whom, and to whom are all things, and He hath most sovereign[44] dominion over all creatures, to do by them, for them, or upon them, whatsoever himself pleaseth; in his sight[45] all things are open and manifest, his knowledge is[46] infinite, infallible, and independent upon the Creature, so as nothing is to Him contingent, or uncertain; He is most holy in all his Councils, in[47] all his Works, and in all his Commands; to Him is due[48] from Angels and men, whatsoever worship, service, or obedience as Creatures they owe unto the Creator, and whatever He is further pleased to require of them.

3. In this divine and infinite Being there are three subsistences,[49] the Father the Word (or Son) and Holy Spirit, of one substance, power, and Eternity, each having the whole Divine Essence,[50] yet the Essence undivided, the Father is of none neither begotten nor proceeding, the Son is[51] Eternally begotten of the Father, the holy Spirit[52] proceeding from the Father and the Son, all infinite, without beginning, therefore but one God, who is not to be divided in nature and Being; but distinguished by several peculiar, relative properties, and personal relations; which doctrine of the Trinity is the foundation of all our Communion with God, and comfortable dependence on him.

[42] *Job, 22.2,3.*
[43] *Rom. 11.34.35,36.*
[44] *Dan. 4.25. and v. 34, 35.*
[45] *Heb. 4.13.*
[46] *Ezek. 11.5 Act. 15.18.*
[47] *Ps. 145.17.*
[48] *Rev. 5.12,13,14.*
[49] *1 Joh. 5.7. Mat. 28.19. 2 Cor. 13.14.*
[50] *Exod. 3.14. Joh. 14.11. 1 Cor. 8.6.*
[51] *Joh. 1.14.18.*
[52] *Joh. 15.26. Gal. 4.6.*

Chapter III

Of God's Decree

1. God hath[53] Decreed in himself from all Eternity, by the most wise and holy Council of his own will, freely and unchangeably, all things whatsoever comes to pass; yet so as thereby is God neither the author of sin,[54] nor hath fellowship with any therein, nor is violence offered to the will of the Creature, nor yet is the liberty, or contingency of second causes taken away, but rather[55] established, in which appears his wisdom in disposing all things, and power, and faithfulness[56] in accomplishing his Decree.

2. Although God knoweth whatsoever may, or can come to pass upon all[57] supposed conditions; yet hath He not Decreed anything,[58] because He foresaw it as future, or as that which would come to pass upon such conditions.

3. By the decree of God for the manifestation of his glory[59] some men and Angels, are predestinated, or fore-ordained to Eternal Life, through Jesus Christ to the[60] praise of his glorious grace; others being left to act in their sin to their[61] just condemnation, to the praise of his glorious justice.

4. These Angels and Men thus predestinated, and fore-ordained, are particularly, and unchangeably designed; and their[62] number so certain, and definite, that it cannot be either increased, or diminished.

---

[53] *Is. 46.10. Eph. 1.11. Heb. 6.17. Rom. 9.15,18.*
[54] *Jam. 1.15,17. 1 Joh. 1.5.*
[55] *Act 4.27,28. Joh. 19.11.*
[56] *Numb. 23.19. Eph. 1.3,4,5.*
[57] *Act. 15.18.*
[58] *Rom. 9.11.13.16.18.*
[59] *1 Tim. 5.21. Mat. 25.41.*
[60] *Eph. 1.5,6.*
[61] *Rom. 9.22,23. Jud. 4.*
[62] *2 Tim. 2.19. Joh. 13.18.*

5. Those of mankind[63] that are predestinated to life, God before the foundation of the world was laid, according to his eternal and immutable purpose, and the secret Council and good pleasure of his will, hath chosen in Christ unto everlasting glory, out of his free grace and love;[64] without any other thing in the creature as a condition or cause moving Him thereunto.

6. As God hath appointed the Elect unto glory, so He hath by the eternal and most free purpose of his will, fore-ordained[65] all the means thereunto, wherefore they who are elected, being fallen in Adam,[66] are redeemed by Christ, are effectually[67] called unto faith in Christ, by his spirit working in due season, are justified, adopted, sanctified, and kept by his power through faith[68] unto salvation; neither are any other redeemed by Christ, or effectually called, justified, adopted, sanctified, and saved, but the Elect[69] only.

7. The Doctrine of this high mystery of predestination, is to be handled with special prudence, and care; that men attending the will of God revealed in his word, and yielding obedience thereunto, may from the certainty of their effectual vocation, be assured of their[70] eternal election; so shall this doctrine afford matter[71] of praise, reverence, and admiration of God, and[72] of humility, diligence, and abundant[73] consolation, to all that sincerely obey the Gospel.

---

[63] *Eph. 1.4.9.11. Rom. 8.30. 2 Tim. 1.9. 1 Thes. 5.9.*
[64] *Rom. 9.13.16. Eph. 1.6.12.*
[65] *1 Pet. 1.2. 2 Thes. 2.13.*
[66] *1 Thes. 5.9,10.*
[67] *Rom. 8.30. 2 Thes. 2.13.*
[68] *1 Pet. 1.5.*
[69] *Joh. 10.26. Joh. 17.9. Joh. 6.64.*
[70] *1 Thes. 1.4,5. 2 Pet. 1.10.*
[71] *Eph. 1.6. Rom. 11.33.*
[72] *Rom. 11.5,6.*
[73] *Luk. 10.20.*

Chapter IV

Of Creation

1. In the beginning it pleased God the Father,[74] Son, and Holy Spirit, for the manifestation of the glory of[75] his eternal power, wisdom, and goodness, to Create or make the world, and all things therein,[76] whether visible or invisible, in the space of six days, and all very good.

2. After God had made all other Creatures, He Created[77] man, male and female, with[78] reasonable and immortal souls, rendering them fit unto that life to God; for which they were Created; being[79] made after the image of God, in knowledge, righteousness, and true holiness; having the Law of God[80] written in their hearts, and power to fulfill it; and yet under a possibility of transgressing, being left to the liberty of their own will, which was[81] subject to change.

3. Besides the Law written in their hearts, they received[82] a command not to eat of the tree of knowledge of good and evil; which whilst they kept, they were happy in their Communion with God, and had dominion[83] over the Creatures.

---

[74] *John 1.2,3. Heb. 1.2. Job 26.13*
[75] *Rom. 1.20.*
[76] *Col. 1.16. Gen 2.1,2.*
[77] *Gen. 1.27.*
[78] *Gen. 2.7.*
[79] *Eccles. 7.29. Gen. 1.26.*
[80] *Rom. 2.14,15.*
[81] *Gen. 3.6.*
[82] *Gen. 6.17. & ch. 3.8,9,10.*
[83] *Gen. 1.26,28.*

Chapter V

Of Divine Providence

1. God the good Creator of all things, in his infinite power, and wisdom, doth[84] uphold, direct, dispose, and govern all Creatures, and things, from the greatest even to the[85] least, by his most wise and holy providence, to the end for the which they were Created; according unto his infallible foreknowledge, and the free and immutable Council of his[86] own will; to the praise of the glory of his wisdom, power, justice, infinite goodness and mercy.

2. Although in relation to the foreknowledge and Decree of God, the first cause, all things come to pass[87] immutably and infallibly; so that there is not anything, befalls any[88] by chance, or without his Providence; yet by the same Providence He ordereth them to fall out, according to the nature of second causes, either[89] necessarily, freely, or contingently.

3. God in his ordinary Providence[90] maketh use of means; yet is free to work, without,[91] above, and[92] against them at his pleasure.

4. The Almighty power, unsearchable wisdom, and infinite goodness of God, so far manifest themselves in his Providence, that his determinate Council[93] extended itself even to the first fall, and all other sinful actions both of Angels, and Men; (and that not by a bare permission) which also He most wisely and powerfully[94] boundeth, and otherwise ordereth, and governeth, in a manifold dispensation to

---

[84] *Heb. 1.3. Job 38.11. Isa. 46 10,11. Ps. 135.6.*
[85] *Mat. 10.29,30,31.*
[86] *Eph. 1.11.*
[87] *Act. 2.23.*
[88] *Pro. 16.33.*
[89] *Gen. 8.22.*
[90] *Act. 27.31.44. Isa. 55.10 11.*
[91] *Rom. 4.19,20,21.*
[92] *Dan. 3.27.*
[93] *Rom. 11 32,33.34. 2 Sam. 24 1. 1 Chro. 21.1.*
[94] *2 Kings 19.28. Ps. 76.10.*

his most holy[95] ends: yet so, as the sinfulness of their acts proceedeth only from the Creatures, and not from God; who being most holy and righteous, neither is nor can be, the author or[96] approver of sin.

5. The most wise, righteous, and gracious God, doth oftentimes, leave for a season his own children to manifold temptations, and the corruptions of their own heart, to chastise them for their former sins, or to discover unto them the hidden strength of corruption, and deceitfulness of their hearts,[97] that they may be humbled; and to raise them to a more close, and constant dependence for their support, upon himself; and to make them more watchful against all future occasions of sin, and for other just and holy ends.

So that whatsoever befalls any of his elect is by his appointment, for his glory,[98] and their good.

6. As for those wicked and ungodly men, whom God as a righteous judge, for former sin doth[99] blind and harden; from them He not only withholdeth his[100] Grace, whereby they might have been enlightened in their understanding, and wrought upon in their hearts: But sometimes also withdraweth[101] the gifts which they had, and exposeth them to such[102] objects as their corruptions makes occasion of sin; and withal[103] gives them over to their own lusts, the temptations of the world, and the power of Satan, whereby it comes to pass, that they[104] harden themselves, even under those means which God useth for the softening of others.

7. As the Providence of God doth in general reach to all Creatures, so after a most special manner it taketh care of his[105] Church, and disposeth of all things to the good thereof.

---

[95] *Gen. 50 20. Isa. 10 6,7.12.*
[96] *Ps. 50.21 1 Joh. 2.16.*
[97] *2 Chro. 32.25,26.31. 2 Sam. 24 1. 2 Cor. 12.7,8,9.*
[98] *Rom. 8.28.*
[99] *Rom. 1.24.26.28. ch. 11.7,8.*
[100] *Deut. 29.4.*
[101] *Mat. 13.12.*
[102] *Deut. 2.30. 2 King. 8.12,13.*
[103] *Psal. 81.11,12. 2 Thes. 2.10,11,12.*
[104] *Exod. 8.15.32. Is. 6.9,10. 1 Pet. 2.7,8.*
[105] *1 Tim. 4.10. Amos 9.8.9. Isa. 43.3,4,5.*

Chapter VI

Of *the* Fall *of* Man, *of* Sin, and *of the* Punishment *thereof*

1. Although God created Man upright, and perfect, and gave him a righteous law, which had been unto life had He kept it, and although God threatened death upon the breach thereof; yet He did not long abide in this honor;[106] Satan using the subtlety of the serpent to seduce Eve, then by her seducing Adam, who without any compulsion, did willfully transgress the Law of their Creation, and the command given unto them, in eating the forbidden fruit; which God was pleased according to his wise and holy Council to permit, having purposed to order it, to his own glory.

2. Our first Parents by this Sin, fell from their[107] original righteousness and communion with God, and we in them, whereby death came upon all;[108] all becoming dead in Sin, and wholly defiled,[109] in all the faculties, and parts, of soul, and body.

3. They being the[110] root, and by Gods appointment, standing in the room, and stead of all mankind; the guilt of the Sin was imputed, and corrupted nature conveyed, to all their posterity descending from them by ordinary generation, being now[111] conceived in Sin, and by nature children[112] of wrath, the servants of Sin, the subjects[113] of death and all other miseries, spiritual, temporal and eternal, unless the Lord Jesus[114] set them free.

---

[106] *Gen. 3.12,13. 2 Cor. 11 3.*

[107] *Rom. 3.23.*

[108] *Rom 5.12 etc.*

[109] *Tit. 1.15 Gen. 6.5. Jer. 17 9. Rom. 3.10-19.*

[110] *Rom. 5.12-19. 1 Cor. 15.21,22.45.49.*

[111] *Ps. 51.5. Job 14.4.*

[112] *Eph. 2.3.*

[113] *Rom. 6.20. & ch. 5.12.*

[114] *Heb. 2.14. 1 Thes. 1.10.*

4. From this original corruption, whereby we are[115] utterly indisposed, disabled, and made opposite to all good, and wholly inclined to all evil.

5. The corruption of nature, during this Life, doth[116] remain in those that are regenerated: and although it be through Christ pardoned, and mortified, yet both itself, and the first motions thereof, are truly and properly[117] sinful.

[115] *Rom. 8.7. Col. 1.21.*
[116] *Rom. 7.18.23. Eccles. 7.20. 1 Joh. 1.8.*
[117] *Rom. 7.24.25. Gal. 5.17.*

Chapter VII

Of God's Covenant

1. The distance between God and the Creature is so great, that although reasonable Creatures do owe obedience unto Him as their Creator, yet they could never have attained the reward of Life, but by some[118] voluntary condescension on Gods part, which He hath been pleased to express, by way of Covenant.

2. Moreover Man having brought himself[119] under the curse of the Law by his fall, it pleased the Lord to make a Covenant of Grace wherein He freely offereth unto Sinners,[120] Life and Salvation by Jesus Christ, requiring of them Faith in him, that they may be saved; and[121] promising to give unto all those that are ordained unto eternal Life, his holy Spirit, to make them willing, and able to believe.

3. This Covenant is revealed in the Gospel; first of all to Adam in the promise of Salvation by the[122] seed of the woman, and afterwards by farther steps, until the full[123] discovery thereof was completed in the new Testament; and it is founded in that[124] Eternal Covenant transaction, that was between the Father and the Son, about the Redemption of the Elect; and it is alone by the Grace of this Covenant, that all of the posterity of fallen Adam, that ever were[125] saved, did obtain life and a blessed immortality; Man being now utterly incapable of acceptance with God upon those terms, on which Adam stood in his state of innocency.

---

[118] *Luk. 17.10. Job 35.7.8.*
[119] *Gen. 2.17. Gal. 3.10. Rom. 3.20,21.*
[120] *Rom. 8.3. Mark 16.15.16. Joh. 3.16.*
[121] *Ezek. 36.26,27. Joh. 6.44 45. Ps. 110.3.*
[122] *Gen. 3.15.*
[123] *Heb. 1.1.*
[124] *2 Tim. 1.9. Tit. 1.2.*
[125] *Heb. 11.6.13. Rom. 4.1,2, etc. Act. 4.12. Joh. 8.56.*

Chapter VIII

Of Christ *the* Mediator

1. It pleased God in his eternal purpose, to choose and ordain the Lord Jesus his only begotten Son, according to the Covenant made between them both,[126] to be the Mediator between God and Man; the[127] Prophet,[128] Priest and[129] King; Head and Savior of his Church, the heir of all things, and judge of the world: Unto whom He did from all Eternity[130] give a people to be his seed, and to be by Him in time redeemed, called, justified, sanctified, and glorified.

2. The Son of God, the second Person in the Holy Trinity, being very and eternal God, the brightness of the Fathers glory, of one substance and equal with him: who made the World, who upholdeth and governeth all things He hath made: did when the fullness of time was come take unto him[131] mans nature, with all the Essential properties, and common infirmities thereof,[132] yet without sin: being conceived by the Holy Spirit in the Womb of the Virgin Mary, the Holy Spirit coming down upon her, and the power of the most High overshadowing her,[133] and so was made of a Woman, of the Tribe of Judah, of the Seed of Abraham, and David according to the Scriptures: So that two whole, perfect, and distinct natures, were inseparably joined together in one Person: without conversion, composition, or confusion: which Person is very God, and very Man; yet one[134] Christ, the only Mediator between God and Man.

---

[126] *Is. 42.1. 1 Pet. 1.19,20.*
[127] *Act. 3.22.*
[128] *Heb. 5.5,6.*
[129] *Ps. 2.6. Luk. 1.33. Eph. 1.23. Heb. 1.2. Act. 17.31.*
[130] *Is. 53.10. Joh. 17.6. Rom. 8:30.*
[131] *Is. 53.10. Joh. 17.6. Rom. 8:30.*
[132] *Rom. 8.3. Heb. 2.14.16,17. ch. 4.15.*
[133] *Luk. 1.27,31.35.*
[134] *Rom. 9.5. 1 Tim. 2.5.*

3. The Lord Jesus in his human nature thus united to the divine, in the Person of the Son, was sanctified, & anointed[135] with the Holy Spirit, above measure; having in him[136] all the treasures of wisdom and knowledge; in whom it pleased the Father that[137] all fullness should dwell: To the end that being[138] holy, harmless, undefiled, and full[139] of Grace, and Truth, He might be thoroughly furnished to execute the office of a[140] Surety; which office He took not upon himself, but was thereunto[141] called by his Father; who also put[142] all power and judgment in his hand, and gave Him Commandment to execute the same.

4. This office the Lord Jesus did most[143] willingly undertake, which that He might discharge he was made under the Law,[144] and did perfectly fulfill it, and underwent the[145] punishment due to us, which we should have born and suffered, being made[146] Sin and a Curse for us: enduring most grievous sorrows[147] in his Soul; and most painful sufferings in his body; was crucified, and died, and remained in the state of the dead; yet saw no[148] corruption: on the[149] third day He arose from the dead, with the same[150] body in which He suffered; with which He also[151] ascended into heaven: and there sitteth at the right hand of his Father,[152] making intercession; and shall[153] return to judge Men and Angels, at the end of the World.

---

135 *Ps. 45.7. Act. 10.38. Joh. 3.34.*
136 *Col. 2.3.*
137 *Col. 1.19.*
138 *Heb. 7.26.*
139 *Joh. 1.14.*
140 *Heb. 7.22.*
141 *Heb. 5.5.*
142 *Joh. 5.22.27. Mat. 28.18. Act. 2.36.*
143 *Ps. 40.7,8. Heb. 10.5-11. Joh. 10.18.*
144 *Gal. 4 4. Mat. 3.15.*
145 *Gal. 3.13. Isa. 53.6. 1 Pet. 3.18.*
146 *2 Cor. 5 21.*
147 *Mat. 26.37,38. Luk. 22.44. Mat. 27.46.*
148 *Act. 13.37.*
149 *1 Cor. 15.3,4.*
150 *Joh. 20.25.27.*
151 *Mark 16 19. Act. 1.9,10,11.*
152 *Rom. 8.34. Heb. 9.24.*
153 *Act. 10.42. Rom. 14.9,10. Act. 1.11.*

5. The Lord Jesus by his perfect obedience and sacrifice of himself, which He through the Eternal Spirit once offered up unto God,[154] hath fully satisfied the Justice of God, procured reconciliation, and purchased an Everlasting inheritance in the Kingdom of Heaven,[155] for all those whom the Father hath given unto him.

6. Although the price of Redemption was not actually paid by Christ, till after his Incarnation,[156] yet the virtue, efficacy, and benefit thereof were communicated to the Elect in all ages successively, from the beginning of the World, in and by those Promises, Types, and Sacrifices, wherein He was revealed, and signified to be the Seed of the Woman, which should bruise the Serpents head;[157] and the Lamb slain from the foundation of the World:[158] Being the same yesterday, and today, and forever.

7. Christ in the work of Mediation acteth according to both natures, by each nature doing that which is proper to itself; yet by reason of the Unity of the Person, that which is proper to one nature, is sometimes in Scripture attributed to the Person[159] denominated by the other nature.

8. To all those for whom Christ hath obtained eternal redemption, He doth certainly, and effectually[160] apply, and communicate the same; making intercession for them, uniting them to himself by his spirit,[161] revealing unto them, in and by the word, the mystery of salvation; persuading them to believe, and obey;[162] governing their hearts by his word and spirit, and[163] overcoming all their enemies by his Almighty power, and wisdom; in such manner, and ways as are most consonant to his wonderful, and[164]

---

154 *Heb. 9.14. ch. 10.14. Rom. 3.25,26.*
155 *Joh. 17.2. Heb. 9.15.*
156 *1 Cor. 4.10. Heb. 4.2. 1 Pet. 1.10,11.*
157 *Rev. 13.8.*
158 *Heb. 13.8.*
159 *Joh. 3.13. Act. 20.28.*
160 *Joh. 6.37. ch. 10.15.16. & ch. 17.9. Rom. 5.10.*
161 *Joh. 17.6. Eph. 1.9. 1 Joh. 5.20.*
162 *Rom. 8.9.14.*
163 *Ps. 110.1. 1 Cor. 15.25,26.*
164 *Joh. 3.8. Eph. 1.8.*

unsearchable dispensation; and all of free, and absolute Grace, without any condition foreseen in them, to procure it.

9. This office of Mediator between God and Man, is proper[165] only to Christ, who is the Prophet, Priest, and King of the Church of God; and may not be either in whole, or any part thereof transferred from Him to any other.

10. This number and order of Offices is necessary; for in respect of our[166] ignorance, we stand in need of his prophetical Office; and in respect of our alienation from God,[167] and imperfection of the best of our services, we need his Priestly office, to reconcile us, and present us acceptable unto God: and in respect o our averseness, and utter inability to return to God, and for our rescue, and security from our spiritual adversaries, we need his Kingly office,[168] to convince, subdue, draw, uphold, deliver, and preserve us to His Heavenly Kingdom.

---

[165] *1 Tim. 2.5.*
[166] *Joh. 1.18.*
[167] *Col. 1.21. Gal. 5.17.*
[168] *Joh. 16.8. Ps. 110.3. Luk. 1.74.75.*

Chapter IX

Of Free Will

1. God hath indued the Will of Man, with that natural liberty, and power of acting upon choice; that it is[169] neither forced, nor by any necessity of nature determined to do good or evil.

2. Man in his state of innocency, had freedom, and power, to will, and to do that[170] which was good, and well-pleasing to God; but yet[171] was mutable, so that He might fall from it.

3. Man by his fall into a state of sin hath wholly lost[172] all ability of Will, to any spiritual good accompanying salvation; so as a natural man, being altogether averse from that good,[173] and dead in Sin, is not able, by his own strength, to[174] convert himself; or to prepare himself thereunto.

4. When God converts a sinner, and translates him into the state of Grace[175] He freeth him from his natural bondage under sin, and by his grace alone, enables him[176] freely to will, and to do that which is spiritually good; yet so as that by reason of his[177] remaining corruptions He doth not perfectly nor only will that which is good; but doth also will that which is evil.

5. The Will of Man is made[178] perfectly, and immutably free to good alone, in the state of glory only.

---

[169] *Mat. 17.12. Jam. 1 14. Deut. 30.19.*
[170] *Eccl. 7.29.*
[171] *Gen. 3.6.*
[172] *Rom. 5.6. ch. 8.7.*
[173] *Eph. 2.1.5.*
[174] *Tit. 3 3,4,5. Joh. 6.44.*
[175] *Col. 1.13. Joh. 8.36.*
[176] *Phil. 2.13.*
[177] *Rom. 7.15.18,19 21.23.*
[178] *Eph. 4.13.*

Chapter X

Of Effectual Calling

1. Those whom God hath predestinated unto Life, He is pleased in his appointed, and accepted time,[179] effectually to call by his word, and Spirit, out of that state of sin, and death, in which they are by nature, to grace and Salvation[180] by Jesus Christ; enlightening their minds, spiritually, and savingly to[181] understand the things of God; taking away their[182] heart of stone, and giving unto them an heart of flesh; renewing their wills, and by his Almighty power determining them[183] to that which is good, and effectually drawing them to Jesus Christ; yet so as they come[184] most freely, being made willing by his Grace.

2. This Effectual Call is of God's free, and special grace alone,[185] not from anything at all foreseen in man, nor from any power, or agency in the Creature, co-working with his special Grace,[186] the Creature being wholly passive therein, being dead in sins and trespasses, until being quickened & renewed by the holy Spirit, He is thereby enabled to answer this call, and to embrace the Grace offered and conveyed in it; and that by no less[187] power, then that which raised up Christ from the dead.

3. Infants dying in infancy, are[188] regenerated and saved by Christ through the Spirit; who worketh when, and where, and[189] how He pleaseth: so also are all other elect persons, who are incapable of being outwardly called by the Ministry of the Word.

---

[179] *Rom. 8.30. Rom. 11.7. Eph. 1.10,11. 2 Thes. 3.13-14.*
[180] *Eph. 2.1-6.*
[181] *Act. 26.18. Eph. 1.17.18.*
[182] *Ezk. 36.26.*
[183] *Deut. 30 6. Ezek. 36.27. Eph. 1.19.*
[184] *Ps. 110.3. Cant. 1.4.*
[185] *2 Tim. 1.9. Eph. 2.8.*
[186] *1 Cor. 2.14. Eph. 2.5. Joh. 5.25.*
[187] *Eph. 1.19,20.*
[188] *Joh. 3.3 5,6.*
[189] *Joh. 3.8.*

4. Others not elected, although they may be called by the Ministry of the word,[190] and may have some common operations of the Spirit, yet not being effectually drawn by the Father, they neither will, nor can truly[191] come to Christ; and therefore cannot be saved: much less can men that receive not the Christian Religion[192] be saved; be they never so diligent to frame their lives according to the light of nature, and the Law of that Religion they do profess.

[190] *Mat. 22 14. ch. 13.20,21. Heb. 6.4,5.*
[191] *John 6.44,45.65. 1 Joh. 2.24,25.*
[192] *Act. 4.12. Joh. 4.22. ch. 17.3.*

Chapter XI

Of Justification

1. Those whom God Effectually calleth, He also freely[193] justified, not by infusing Righteousness into them, but by[194] pardoning their sins, and by accounting, and accepting their Persons as[195] Righteous; not for anything wrought in them, or done by them, but for Christ's sake alone, not by imputing faith itself, the act of believing, or any other[196] evangelical obedience to them, as their Righteousness; but by imputing Christ's active obedience unto the whole Law, and passive obedience in his death, for their whole and sole Righteousness, they[197] receiving, and resting on him, and his Righteousness, by Faith; which faith they have not of themselves, it is the gift of God.

2. Faith thus receiving and resting on Christ, and his Righteousness, is the[198] alone instrument of Justification: yet it is not alone in the person justified, but is ever accompanied with all other saving Graces, and is no dead faith,[199] but worketh by love.

3. Christ by his obedience, and death, did fully discharge the debt of all ; and did by the sacrifice of himself, in the blood of his cross, undergoing in their stead, the penalty due unto them: make a proper, real and full satisfaction[200] to Gods justice in their behalf: yet in as much as He was given by the Father for them, and his Obedience and Satisfaction accepted in their stead, and both[201] freely, not for anything in them; their Justification is only of Free

---

[193] *Rom. 3.24. ch. 8.30.*
[194] *Rom. 4.5,6,7,8. Eph. 1.7.*
[195] *1 Cor. 1.30,31. Rom. 5.17 18,19.*
[196] *Phil. 3.8,9. Eph. 2.8,9,10.*
[197] *Joh. 1.12. Rom. 5.17.*
[198] *Rom. 3.28.*
[199] *Gal. 5.6. Jam. 2.17 22.26.*
[200] *Heb. 10.14. 1 Pet. 1.18,19. Isa. 53.5,6.*
[201] *Rom. 8.32. 2 Cor. 5.21.*

Grace, that both the exact justice and rich Grace of God, might be[202] glorified in the Justification of sinners.

4. God did from all eternity decree to[203] justify all the Elect, and Christ did in the fullness of time die for their sins, and rise[204] again for their Justification; Nevertheless they are not justified personally, until the Holy Spirit, doth in due time[205] actually apply Christ unto them.

5. God continues to[206] Forgive the sins of those who are justified, and although they can never fall from the state of[207] justification; yet they may by their sins fall under God's[208] Fatherly displeasure; and in that condition, they have not usually the light of his Countenance restored unto them, until they[209] humble themselves, confess their sins, beg pardon, and renew their faith, and repentance.

6. The Justification of Believers under the Old Testament was in all these respects,[210] one and the same with the justification of Believers under the New Testament.

---

[202] *Rom. 3.26. Eph. 1 6,7. ch. 2.7.*
[203] *Gal. 3.8. 1 Pet. 1.2. 1 Tim. 2.6.*
[204] *Rom. 4.25.*
[205] *Col. 1.21,22. Tit. 3.4,5,6,7.*
[206] *Mat. 6.12. 1 John 1.7.9.*
[207] *Joh. 10 28.*
[208] *Ps. 89.31,32,33.*
[209] *Psal. 32:5. & 51. Mat. 26.75.*
[210] *Gal. 3.9. Rom. 4.22,23,24.*

Chapter XII

Of Adoption

1. All those that are justified, God vouchsafed, in, and for the sake of his only Son Jesus Christ, to make partakers of the Grace[211] of Adoption; by which they are taken into the number, and enjoy the Liberties, and[212] Privileges of Children of God; have his[213] name put upon them,[214] receive the Spirit of Adoption,[215] have access to the throne of Grace with boldness, are enabled to cry Abba, Father, are[216] pitied,[217] protected,[218] provided for, and[219] chastened by him, as by a Father; yet never[220] cast off; but sealed[221] to the day of Redemption, and inherit the promises,[222] as heirs, of everlasting Salvation.

---

[211] *Eph. 1.5. Gal. 4.4,5.*
[212] *Joh. 1.12. Rom. 8.17.*
[213] *2 Cor. 6.18. Rev. 3.12.*
[214] *Rom. 8.15.*
[215] *Gal. 4.6. Eph. 2.18.*
[216] *Ps. 103.13.*
[217] *Prov. 14 26.*
[218] *1 Pet. 5.7.*
[219] *Heb. 12.6.*
[220] *Is. 54.8,9. Lam. 3.31.*
[221] *Eph. 4.30.*
[222] *Heb. 1.14. ch. 6.12.*

Chapter XIII

Of Sanctification

1. They who are united to Christ, effectually called, and regenerated, having a new heart, and a new Spirit created in them, through the virtue of Christ's death, and Resurrection; are also[223] farther sanctified, really, and personally, through the same virtue,[224] by his word and Spirit dwelling in them;[225] the dominion of the whole body of sin is destroyed,[226] and the several lusts thereof, are more and more weakened, and mortified; and they more and more quickened, and[227] strengthened in all saving graces, to the[228] practice of all true holiness, without which no man shall see the Lord.

2. This Sanctification is[229] throughout, in the whole man, yet imperfect[230] in this life; there abideth still some remnants of corruption in every part, whence ariseth a[231] continual, and irreconcilable war; the Flesh lusting against the Spirit, and the Spirit against the Flesh.

3. In which war, although the remaining corruption for a time may much[232] prevail; yet through the continual supply of strength from the sanctifying Spirit of Christ the[233] regenerate part doth overcome; and so the Saints grow in Grace, perfecting holiness in the fear of God,[234] pressing after an heavenly life, in Evangelical Obedience to all the commands which Christ as Head and King, in his Word hath prescribed to them.

---

[223] *Act. 20.32. Rom. 6.5,6.*
[224] *Joh. 17.17. Eph. 3.16,17,18,19. 1 Thes. 5.21,22,23.*
[225] *Rom. 6.14.*
[226] *Gal. 5.24.*
[227] *Col 1.11.*
[228] *2 Cor. 7.1. Heb. 12.14.*
[229] *1 Thes. 5.23.*
[230] *Rom. 7.18,23.*
[231] *Gal. 5.17. 1 Pet. 2.11.*
[232] *Rom. 7.23.*
[233] *Rom. 6.14.*
[234] *Eph. 4.15.16. 2 Cor. 3.18. ch. 7.1.*

Chapter XIV

Of Saving Faith

1. The Grace of Faith, whereby the Elect are enabled to believe to the saving of their souls, is the work of the Spirit of Christ[235] in their hearts; and is ordinarily wrought by the Ministry of the[236] Word; by which also, and by the administration of Baptism, and the Lords Supper, Prayer and other Means appointed of God, it is increased,[237] and strengthened.

2. By this Faith, a Christian believeth to be true,[238] whatsoever is revealed in the Word, for the Authority of God himself; and also apprehended an excellence therein,[239] above all other Writings; and all things in the world: as it bears forth the Glory of God in his Attributes, the excellence of Christ in his Nature and Offices; and the Power and Fullness of the Holy Spirit in his Workings, and Operations; and so is enabled to[240] cast his Soul upon the truth thus believed; and also acted differently, upon that which each particular, passage thereof containeth; yielding obedience to the[241] commands, trembling at the[242] threatening, and embracing the[243] promises of God, for this life, and that which is to come: But the principal acts of Saving Faith, have immediate relation to Christ, accepting, receiving, and resting upon[244] Him alone, for Justification, Sanctification, and Eternal Life, by virtue of the Covenant of Grace.

3. This Faith although it be different in degrees, and may be weak,[245] or strong; yet it is in the least degree of it, different in the

---

[235] 2 Cor. 4.13. Eph. 2.8.
[236] Rom. 10 14.17.
[237] Luk. 17.5. 1 Pet. 2.2. Act. 20.32.
[238] Act. 24.14.
[239] Ps. 19.7,8,9,10. Ps. 119.72.
[240] 2 Tim. 1.12.
[241] Joh. 15.14.
[242] Is. 66.2.
[243] Heb. 11.13.
[244] Joh. 1.12. Act. 16 31. Gal. 2.20. Act. 15.11.
[245] Heb. 5.13.14. Mat. 6.30. Rom. 4.19 20.

kind, or nature of it (as is all other saving Grace) from the Faith,[246] and common grace of temporary believers; and therefore though it may be many times assailed, and weakened; yet it gets[247] the victory; growing up in many, to the attainment of a full[248] assurance through Christ, who is both the Author [249] and finisher of our Faith.

---

[246] *2 Pet. 1.1.*
[247] *Eph. 6.16. 1 Joh. 5.4,5.*
[248] *Heb. 6.11,12. Col. 2.2.*
[249] *Heb. 12.2.*

Chapter XV

Of Repentance *unto* Life *and* Salvation

1. Such of the Elect as are converted at riper years, having[250] sometimes lived in the state of nature, and therein served divers lusts and pleasures, God in their Effectual Calling giveth them Repentance unto Life.

2. Whereas there is none that doth good, and sinneth[251] not; and the best of men may through the power, and deceitfulness of their corruption dwelling in them, with the prevalence of temptation, fall into great sins, and provocations; God hath in the Covenant of Grace, mercifully provided that Believers so sinning, and falling,[252] be renewed through Repentance unto Salvation.

3. This saving Repentance is an[253] evangelical Grace, whereby a person being by the Holy Spirit made sensible of the manifold evils of his sin, doth, by Faith in Christ, humble himself for it, with godly sorrow, detestation of it, and self abhorrence;[254] praying for pardon, and strength of grace, with a purpose and endeavor by supplies of the Spirit, to[255] walk before God unto all well pleasing in all things.

4. As Repentance is to be continued through the whole course of our lives, upon the account of the body of death, and the motions thereof; so it is every man's duty, to repent of his[256] particular known sins, particularly.

5. Such is the provision which God hath made through Christ in the Covenant of Grace, for the preservation of Believers unto Salvation, that although there is no sin so small, but it deserves[257] damnation; yet there is no sin so great, that it shall bring damnation

---

250 *Tit. 3.2,3,4,5.*
251 *Eccl. 7.20.*
252 *Luk. 22.31,32.*
253 *Zech. 12.10. Act. 11.18.*
254 *Ezek. 36.31. 2 Cor. 7.11.*
255 *Ps. 119 6. Ps. 119.128.*
256 *Luk. 19.8. 1 Tim. 1.13.15.*
257 *Rom. 6.23.*

on them that[258] repent; which makes the constant preaching of Repentance necessary.

Chapter XVI

Of Good Works

1. Good Works are only such as God hath[259] commanded in his Holy word; and not such as without the warrant thereof, are devised by men, out of blind zeal,[260] or upon any pretence of good intentions.

2. These good works, done in obedience to Gods commandments, are the fruits, and evidences[261] of a true, and lively faith; and by them Believers manifest their[262] thankfulness, strengthen their[263] assurance, edify their[264] brethren, adorn the profession of the Gospel, stop the mouths of the adversaries and glorify[265] God whose workmanship they are, created in Christ Jesus[266] thereunto, that having their fruit unto holiness, they may have the end[267] eternal life.

3. Their ability to do good works, is not at all of themselves; but wholly from the Spirit[268] of Christ; and that they may be enabled thereunto, besides the graces they have already received, there is necessary an[269] actual influence of the same Holy Spirit, to work in them to will, and to do, of his good pleasure; yet are they not hereupon to grow negligent, as if they were not bound to perform any duty, unless upon a special motion of the Spirit; but they ought to be diligent in[270] stirring up the Grace of God that is in them.

4. They who in their obedience attain to the greatest height which is possible in this life, are so far from being able to

---

[259] *Mic. 6.8. Heb. 13 21.*
[260] *Mat. 15.9. Isa. 29.13.*
[261] *Jam. 2.18.22.*
[262] *Ps. 116.12,13.*
[263] *1 Joh. 2 3.5. 2 Pet. 1.5-11.*
[264] *Mat. 5.16.*
[265] *1 Tim. 6.1. 1 Pet. 2.15. Phil. 1.11.*
[266] *Eph. 2.10.*
[267] *Rom. 6.22.*
[268] *Joh. 15.4.6.*
[269] *2 Cor. 3.5. Phil. 2.13.*
[270] *Phil. 2.12. Heb. 6.11 12. Isa. 64.7.*

supererogate, and to do more than God requires, as that[271] they fall short of much which in duty they are bound to do.

5. We cannot by our best works merit pardon of Sin or Eternal Life at the hand of God, by reason of the great disproportion that is between them and the glory to come; and the infinite distance that is between us and God, whom by them we can neither profit, nor satisfy for the debt of our[272] former sins; but when we have done all we can, we have done but our duty, and are unprofitable servants; and because as they are good they proceed from his[273] Spirit, and as they are wrought by us they are defiled[274] and mixed with so much weakness and imperfection that they cannot endure the severity of Gods judgment.

6. Yet notwithstanding the persons of Believers being accepted through Christ their good works also are accepted in[275] him; not as though they were in this life wholly unblameable and unreprovable in Gods sight; but that He looking upon them in his Son is pleased to accept and reward that which is[276] sincere although accompanied with many weaknesses and imperfections.

7. Works done by unregenerate men although for the matter of them they may be things which God commands, and of good use, both to themselves and[277] others; yet because they proceed not from a heart purified by[278] faith, nor are done in a right manner according to the[279] word, nor to a right end the[280] glory of God; they are therefore sinful and cannot please God; nor make a man meet to receive grace from[281] God; and yet their neglect of them is more sinful and[282] displeasing to God.

---

271 *Job 9.2 3. Gal. 5.17. Luk. 17.10.*
272 *Rom. 3.20. Eph. 2.8,9. Rom. 4.6.*
273 *Gal. 5.22,23.*
274 *Isa. 64.6. Ps. 143 2.*
275 *Eph. 1.6. 1 Pet. 2.5.*
276 *Mat. 25.21.23. Heb. 6.10.*
277 *2 King. 10.30. 1 King. 21.27,29.*
278 *Gen. 4.5. Heb. 11 4.6.*
279 *1 Cor. 13.1.*
280 *Mat. 6.2.5.*
281 *Amos 5 21,22. Rom. 9.16. Tit. 3.5.*
282 *Job 21.14,15. Mat. 25.41,42,43*

Chapter XVII

Of Perseverance *of the* Saints

1. Those whom God hath accepted in the beloved, effectually called and Sanctified by his Spirit, and given the precious faith of his Elect unto, can neither totally nor finally fall from the state of grace;[283] but shall certainly persevere therein to the end and be eternally saved, seeing the gifts and callings of God are without Repentance, (whence He still begets and nourished in them Faith, Repentance, Love, Joy, Hope, and all the graces of the Spirit unto immortality) and though many storms and floods arise and beat against them, yet they shall never be able to take them off that foundation and rock which by faith they are fastened upon: notwithstanding through unbelief and the temptations of Satan the sensible sight of the light and love of God, may for a time be clouded, and obscured from[284] them, yet He is still the same[285] and they shall be sure to be kept by the power of God unto Salvation, where they shall enjoy their purchased possession, they being engraved upon the palm of his hands, and their names having been written in the book of life from all Eternity.

2. This perseverance of the Saints depends not upon their own free will; but upon the immutability of the decree of[286] Election flowing from the free and unchangeable love of God the Father; upon the efficacy of the merit and intercession of Jesus Christ[287] and Union with him, the[288] oath of God, the abiding of his Spirit & the[289] seed of God within them, and the nature of the[290] Covenant of Grace from all which ariseth also the certainty and infallibility thereof.

---

[283] *Joh. 10.28,29. Phi. 1.6. 2 Tim. 2.19. 1 Joh. 2.19.*
[284] *Psal. 89.31,32. 1 Cor. 11.32.*
[285] *Mal. 3.6.*
[286] *Rom. 8.30. ch. 9.11.16.*
[287] *Rom. 5.9,10. John 14.19.*
[288] *Heb. 6.17,18.*
[289] *1 Joh. 3.9.*
[290] *Jer. 32.40.*

3. And though they may through the temptation of Satan and of the world, the prevalence of corruption remaining in them, and the neglect of means of their preservation fall into grievous[291] sins, and for a time continue therein; whereby they incur[292] Gods displeasure, and grieve his holy Spirit, come to have their graces and[293] comforts impaired have their hearts hardened, and their Consciences wounded,[294] hurt, and scandalize others, and bring temporal judgments[295] upon themselves: yet they shall renew their[296] repentance and be preserved through faith in Christ Jesus to the end.

---

[291] *Mat. 26.70,72.74.*
[292] *Is. 64.5.9. Eph. 4.30.*
[293] *Psal. 51.10.12.*
[294] *Psa. 32.3,4.*
[295] *2 Sam. 12.14.*
[296] *Luk. 22.32. & v. 61 62.*

Chapter XVIII

Of *the* Assurance *of* Grace *and* Salvation

1. Although temporary Believers, and other unregenerate men, may vainly deceive themselves with false hopes, and carnal presumptions, of being in the favor of God, and state of salvation,[297] which hope of theirs shall perish; yet such as truly believe in the Lord Jesus, and love Him in sincerity, endeavoring to walk in all good Conscience before him, may in this life be certainly assured[298] that they are in the state of Grace; and may rejoice in the hope of the glory of God which hope shall never make them[299] ashamed.

2. This certainty is not a bare conjectural, and probable persuasion, grounded upon[300] a fallible hope; but an infallible assurance of faith founded on the Blood and Righteousness of Christ[301] revealed in the Gospel; and also upon the inward[302] evidence of those graces of the Spirit unto which promises are made, and on the testimony of the[303] Spirit of adoption, witnessing with our Spirits that we are the children of God; and as a fruit thereof keeping the heart both[304] humble and holy.

3. This infallible assurance doth not so belong to the essence of faith, but that a true Believer, may wait long and conflict with many difficulties before He be[305] partaker of it; yet being enabled by the Spirit to know the things which are freely given him of God, He may without extraordinary revelation in the right use of means[306] attain thereunto: and therefore it is the duty of every one, to give all

---

[297] *Job 8.13.14. Mat. 7.22 23.*
[298] *1 Joh. 2.3. ch. 3.14 18,19.21.24. ch. 5.13.*
[299] *Rom. 5.2.5.*
[300] *Heb. 6.11.19.*
[301] *Heb. 6.17,18.*
[302] *2 Pet. 1.4,5,10.11.*
[303] *Rom. 8.15,16.*
[304] *1 Joh. 3 1,2,3.*
[305] *Isa. 50.10. Ps. 88. & Psa. 77.1-12.*
[306] *1 Joh. 4 13. Heb. 6.11 12.*

diligence to make their Calling and Election sure, that thereby his heart may be enlarged in peace and joy in the holy Spirit, in love and thankfulness to God, and in strength and cheerfulness in the duties of obedience, the proper[307] fruits of this Assurance; so far is it[308] from inclining men to looseness.

4. True Believers may have the assurance of their Salvation divers ways shaken, diminished, and intermitted; as[309] by negligence in preserving of it, by[310] falling into some special Sin, which wounded the Conscience, and grieveth the Spirit, by some sudden or[311] vehement temptation, by Gods withdrawing the[312] light of his countenance and suffering even such as fear Him to walk in darkness and to have no light; yet are they never destitute of the[313] seed of God, and Life[314] of Faith, that Love of Christ, and the brethren, that sincerity of Heart, and Conscience of duty, out of which by the operation of the Spirit, this Assurance may in due time be[315] revived: and by the which in the mean time they are[316] preserved from utter despair.

---

[307] *Rom. 5.1,2.5. ch. 14,17. Ps. 119.32.*
[308] *Rom. 6.1,2. Tit. 2.11,12.14.*
[309] *Cant. 5.2,3.6.*
[310] *Ps. 51.8.12.14.*
[311] *Psa. 116.11. Ps. 77.7,8. Ps. 31 22.*
[312] *Ps. 30.7.*
[313] *1 Joh. 3.9.*
[314] *Luk. 22.32.*
[315] *Ps. 42.5.11.*
[316] *Lam. 3.26.27-31.*

Chapter XIX

Of *the* Law *of* God

1. God gave to Adam a Law of universal obedience,[317] written in his Heart, and a particular precept of not eating the Fruit of the tree of knowledge of good and evil; by which He bound him, and all his posterity to personal entire exact and perpetual[318] obedience; promised life upon the fulfilling, and[319] threatened death upon the breach of it; and endued him with power and ability to keep it.

2. The same Law that was first written in the heart of man,[320] continued to be a perfect rule of Righteousness after the fall; & was delivered by God upon Mount Sinai, in[321] Ten Commandments and written in two Tables; the four first containing our duty towards God, and the other six our duty to man.

3. Besides this Law commonly called moral, God was pleased to give to the people of Israel Ceremonial Laws, containing several typical ordinances, partly of worship,[322] prefiguring Christ, his graces, actions, sufferings, and benefits; and partly holding forth divers instructions[323] of moral duties, all which Ceremonial Laws being appointed only to the time of reformation, are by Jesus Christ the true Messiah and only Law-giver who was furnished with power from the Father, for that end,[324] abrogated and taken away.

4. To them also He gave sundry judicial Laws, which expired together with the state of that people, not obliging any now by virtue of that institution; their general[325] equity only, being of moral use.

---

[317] *Gen. 1.27. Eccl. 7.29.*
[318] *Rom. 10 5.*
[319] *Gal. 3.10.12.*
[320] *Rom. 2.14,15.*
[321] *Deut. 10.4.*
[322] *Heb. 10.1. Col. 2.17.*
[323] *1 Cor. 5 7.*
[324] *Col. 2.14,16,17. Eph. 2.14.16.*
[325] *1 Cor. 9.8,9,10.*

5. The moral Law doth for ever bind all,[326] as well justified persons as others, to the obedience thereof, and that not only in regard of the matter contained in it, but also in respect of the[327] authority of God the Creator; who gave it: Neither doth Christ in the Gospel any way dissolve,[328] but much strengthen this obligation.

6. Although true Believers be not under the Law, as a Covenant of Works,[329] to be thereby Justified or condemned; yet it is of great use to them as well as to others: in that, as a Rule of Life, informing them of the Will of God, and their Duty, it directs and binds them, to walk accordingly;[330] discovering also the sinful pollutions of their Natures, Hearts and Lives; so as Examining themselves thereby, they may come to further Conviction of, Humiliation for, and Hatred against Sin; together with a clearer sight of the need they have of Christ and the perfection of his Obedience: It is likewise of use to the Regenerate to restrain their Corruptions, in that it forbids Sin; and the Threatening of it serve to show what even their Sins deserve; and what afflictions in this Life they may expect for them, although freed from the Curse and undiminished rigor thereof. The Promises of it likewise show them Gods approbation of Obedience, and what blessings they may expect upon the performance thereof, though not as due to them by the Law as a Covenant of Works; so as mans doing Good and refraining from Evil, because the Law encouraged to the one and deterred from the other, is no Evidence of his being[331] under the Law and not under Grace.

7. Neither are the aforementioned uses of the Law[332] contrary to the Grace of the Gospel; but do sweetly comply with it; the Spirit of Christ subduing[333] and enabling the Will of man, to do that freely and cheerfully, which the will of God revealed in the Law, requireth to be done.

---

[326] *Rom. 13 8,9,10. Jam. 2.8.10,11,12.*
[327] *Jam. 2 10,11.*
[328] *Mat. 5.17,18,19. Rom. 3.31.*
[329] *Rom. 6.14. Gal. 2.16. Rom. 8.1. chap. 10.4.*
[330] *Rom. 3.20. chap. 7.7. etc.*
[331] *Rom. 6.12,13,14. 1 Pet. 3.8.-13.*
[332] *Gal. 3.21.*
[333] *Eze. 36.27.*

Chapter XX

Of *the* Gospel,
and of the Extent *of the* Grace *thereof*

1. The Covenant of Works being broken by Sin, and made unprofitable unto Life; God was pleased to give forth the promise of Christ,[334] the Seed of the Woman, as the means of calling the Elect, and begetting in them Faith and Repentance; in this Promise, the[335] Gospel, as to the substance of it, was revealed, and therein Effectual, for the Conversion and Salvation of Sinners.

2. This Promise of Christ, and Salvation by him, is revealed only by[336] the Word of God; neither do the Works of Creation, or Providence, with the light of Nature,[337] make discovery of Christ, or of Grace by him; so much as in a general, or obscure way; much less that men destitute of the Revelation of Him by the Promise, or Gospel;[338] should be enabled thereby, to attain saving Faith, or Repentance.

3. The Revelation of the Gospel unto Sinners, made in divers times, and by sundry parts; with the addition of Promises, and Precepts for the Obedience required therein, as to the Nations, and Persons, to whom it is granted, is merely of the[339] Sovereign Will and good Pleasure of God; not being annexed by virtue of any Promise, to the due improvement of men's natural abilities, by virtue of Common light received, without it; which none ever did[340] make, or can so do: And therefore in all Ages the preaching of the Gospel hath been granted unto persons and Nations, as to the extent, or

---

334 *Gen. 3.15.*
335 *Rev. 13.8.*
336 *Rom. 1.17.*
337 *Rom. 10.14,15,17.*
338 *Pro. 29.18. Isa. 25.7. with ch. 60.2,3.*
339 *Ps. 147,20. Act. 16.7.*
340 *Rom. 1.18, etc.*

straightening of it, in great variety, according to the Council of the Will of God.

4. Although the Gospel be the only outward means, of revealing Christ, and saving Grace; and is, as such, abundantly sufficient thereunto; yet that men who are dead in Trespasses, may be born again, Quickened or Regenerated; there is moreover necessary, an effectual, insuperable[341] work of the Holy Spirit, upon the whole Soul, for the producing in them a new spiritual Life; without which no other means will affect[342] their Conversion unto God.

---

[341] *Ps. 110.3. 1 Cor. 2.14. Eph. 1.19 20.*
[342] *Joh. 6.44. 2 Cor. 4.4.6.*

Chapter XXI

Of Christian Liberty *and*
Liberty *of* Conscience

1. The Liberty which Christ hath purchased for Believers under the Gospel, consists in their freedom from the guilt of Sin, the condemning wrath of God, the rigors and[343] Curse of the Law; and in their being delivered from this present evil[344] World, Bondage to[345] Satan, and Dominion[346] of Sin; from the[347] Evil of Afflictions; the Fear, and Sting[348] of Death, the Victory of the Grave, and[349] Everlasting Damnation; as also in their[350] free access to God; and their yielding Obedience unto Him not out of a slavish fear,[351] but a Child-like love, and willing mind.

All which were common also to Believers under the Law[352] for the substance of them; but under the new Testament, the Liberty of Christians is further enlarged in their freedom from the yoke of the Ceremonial Law, to which the Jewish Church was subjected; and in greater boldness of access to the Throne of Grace; and in fuller Communications of the[353] Free Spirit of God, then Believers under the Law did ordinarily partake of.

2. God alone is[354] Lord of the Conscience, and hath left it free from the Doctrines and Commandments of men,[355] which are in anything contrary to his Word, or not contained in it. So that to

---

[343] *Gal. 3.13.*
[344] *Gal. 1.4.*
[345] *Act. 26.18.*
[346] *Rom. 8.3.*
[347] *Rom. 8.28.*
[348] *1 Cor. 15.54,55,56.57.*
[349] *2 Thes. 1.10.*
[350] *Rom. 8.15.*
[351] *Luk. 1.74,75. 1 Joh. 4 18.*
[352] *Gal. 3,9:14.*
[353] *Joh. 7.38,39. Heb. 10, 19,20,21.*
[354] *Jam. 4.12. Rom. 14.4.*
[355] *Act. 4.19 & 5.29. 1 Cor. 7.23. Mat. 15.9.*

Believe such Doctrines, or obey such Commands out of Conscience,[356] is to betray true liberty of Conscience; and the requiring of an[357] implicit Faith, and absolute and blind Obedience, is to destroy Liberty of Conscience, and Reason also.

3. They who upon pretence of Christian Liberty do practice any sin, or cherish any sinful lust; as they do thereby pervert the main design of the Grace of the Gospel,[358] to their own Destruction; so they wholly destroy[359] the end of Christian Liberty, which is, that being delivered out of the hands of all our Enemies we might serve the Lord without fear in Holiness, and Righteousness before him, all the days of our Life.

[356] *Col. 2.20 22,23.*
[357] *1 Cor. 3.5. 2 Cor. 1.24.*
[358] *Rom. 6.1,2.*
[359] *Gal. 5.13. 2 Pet. 2.18.-21.*

Chapter XXII

Of Religious Worship *and the* Sabbath Day

1. The light of Nature shows that there is a God, who hath Lordship, and Sovereignty over all; is just, good, and doth good unto all; and is therefore to be feared, loved, praised, called upon, trusted in, and served, with all the Heart, and all the Soul,[360] and with all the Might. But the acceptable way of Worshipping the true God, is[361] instituted by himself; and so limited by his own revealed will, that He may not be Worshipped according to the imaginations, and devices of Men, or the suggestions of Satan, under any visible representations, or[362] any other way, not prescribed in the Holy Scriptures.

2. Religious Worship is to be given to God the Father, Son, and Holy Spirit, and to him[363] alone; not to Angels, Saints, or any other[364] Creatures; and since the fall, not without a[365] Mediator, nor in the Mediation of any other but[366] Christ alone.

3. Prayer with thanksgiving, being one special part of natural worship, is by God required of[367] all men. But that it may be accepted, it is to be made in the[368] Name of the Son, by the help[369] of the Spirit, according to[370] his Will; with understanding, reverence, humility, fervency, faith, love, and perseverance; and when with others, in a[371] known tongue.

---

[360] *Jer. 10.7. Mar. 12.33.*
[361] *Deut. 12 32.*
[362] *Exo 20.4,5,6.*
[363] *Mat. 4.9,10. Joh 6.23. Mat. 28.19.*
[364] *Rom. 1.25. Col. 2.18. Revel. 19.10.*
[365] *Joh. 14.6.*
[366] *1 Tim. 2.5.*
[367] *Psal. 95 1-7. Psal. 65.2.*
[368] *Joh. 14.13,14.*
[369] *Rom. 8.26.*
[370] *1 Joh. 5.14.*
[371] *1 Cor. 14.16,17.*

4. Prayer is to be made for things lawful, and for all sorts of men living,[372] or that shall live hereafter; but not[373] for the dead, nor for those of whom it may be known that they have sinned[374] the sin unto death.

5. The[375] reading of the Scriptures, Preaching, and[376] hearing the word of God, teaching and admonishing one another in Psalms, Hymns and Spiritual songs, singing with grace in our Hearts to[377] the Lord; as also the Administration[378] of Baptism, and[379] the Lords Supper are all parts of Religious worship of God, to be performed in obedience to him, with understanding, faith, reverence, and godly fear; moreover solemn humiliation[380] with fastings; and thanksgiving upon[381] special occasions, ought to be used in an holy and religious manner.

6. Neither Prayer, nor any other part of Religious worship, is now under the Gospel tied unto, or made more acceptable by, any place in which it is[382] performed, or towards which it is directed; but God is to be worshipped everywhere in Spirit, and in truth; as in[383] private families[384] daily, and[385] in secret each one by himself, so more solemnly in the public Assemblies, which are not carelessly, nor willfully, to be[386] neglected, or forsaken, when God by his word, or providence calleth thereunto.

7. As it is of the Law of nature, that in general a proportion of time by Gods appointment, be set apart for the Worship of God; so by his Word in a positive-moral, and perpetual Commandment,

---

372 *1 Tim. 2.1,2. 2 Sam. 7.29.*
373 *2 Sam. 12.21,22.23.*
374 *1 Joh. 5.16.*
375 *1 Tim. 4.13.*
376 *2 Tim. 4.2. Luk. 8.18.*
377 *Col. 3.16. Eph. 5.19.*
378 *Mat. 28, 19,20.*
379 *1 Cor. 11 26.*
380 *Esth. 4.16. Joel. 2.12.*
381 *Exo. 15.1. etc. Ps. 107.*
382 *Joh. 4.21. Mal. 1.11. 1 Tim 2.8.*
383 *Act. 10.2.*
384 *Mat. 6.11. Ps. 55.17.*
385 *Mat. 6.6.*
386 *Heb. 10.25. Act. 2.42.*

binding all men, in all Ages, He hath particularly appointed one day in seven for a[387] Sabbath to be kept holy unto him, which from the beginning of the World to the Resurrection of Christ, was the last day of the week; and from the resurrection of Christ, was changed into the first day of the week[388] which is called the Lords day; and is to be continued to the end of the World, as the Christian Sabbath; the observation of the last day of the week being abolished.

8. The Sabbath is then kept holy unto the Lord, when men after a due preparing of their hearts, and ordering their common affairs, do not only observe an holy[389] rest all the day, from their own works, words, and thoughts, about their worldly employment, and recreations, but also are taken up the whole time in the public and private exercises of his worship, and in the duties[390] of necessity and mercy.

---

387 *Exo. 20.8.*
388 *1 Cor. 16.1,2. Act. 20.7. Rev. 1.10.*
389 *Isa. 58.13. Neh 13.15-23.*
390 *Mat. 12.1-13.*

Chapter XXIII

Of Lawful Oaths *and* Vows

1. A lawful Oath is a part of religious worship,[391] wherein the person swearing in Truth, Righteousness, and Judgment, solemnly calleth God to witness what He sweareth;[392] and to judge him according to the Truth or falseness thereof.

2. The Name of God only is that by which men ought to swear; and therein it is to be used, with all Holy Fear and reverence, therefore to swear vainly or rashly by that glorious, and dreadful name; or to swear at all by any other thing, is sinful and to be[393] abhorred; yet as in matter of weight and moment for confirmation of truth,[394] and ending all strife, an Oath is warranted by the Word of God; so a lawful Oath being imposed,[395] by lawful Authority, in such matters, ought to be taken.

3. Whosoever taketh an Oath warranted by the Word of God, ought duly to consider the weightiness of so solemn an act; and therein to avouch nothing, but what He knoweth to be the truth; for that by rash, false, and vain Oaths the[396] Lord is provoked, and for them this Land mourns.

4. An Oath is to be taken in the plain, and[397] common sense of the words; without equivocation, or mental reservation.

5. A Vow which is not to be made to any Creature, but to God alone,[398] is to be made and performed with all Religious care, and faithfulness: But Popish Monastical Vows,[399] of perpetual single life,

---

[391] *Exo. 20 7. Deut. 10 20. Jer. 4.2.*
[392] *2 Cro. 6 22,23.*
[393] *Mat. 5.34.37. Jam. 5.12.*
[394] *Heb. 6.16. 2 Cor. 1.23.*
[395] *Neh. 13.25.*
[396] *Levit. 19.12. Jer. 23.10.*
[397] *Ps. 24.4.*
[398] *Psal. 76.11. Gen. 28.20,21 22.*
[399] *1 Cor. 7.2.9.*

professed[400] poverty, and regular obedience, are so far from being degrees of higher perfection, that they are superstitious,[401] and sinful snares, in which no Christian may entangle himself.

---

[400] *Eph. 4.28.*
[401] *Mat. 19.11.*

Chapter XXIV

Of *the* Civil Magistrate

1. God the supreme Lord, and King of all the World, hath ordained Civil[402] Magistrates to be under him, over the people for his own glory, and the public good; and to this end hath armed them with the power of the Sword, for defense and encouragement of them that do good, and for the punishment of evil doers.

2. It is lawful for Christians to Accept, and Execute the Office of a Magistrate when called thereunto; in the management whereof, as they ought especially to maintain[403] Justice, and Peace, according to the wholesome Laws of each Kingdome, and Commonwealth: so for that end they may lawfully now under the New Testament[404] wage war upon just and necessary occasions.

3. Civil Magistrates being set up by God, for the ends aforesaid; subjection in all lawful things commanded by them, ought to be yielded by us, in the Lord; not only for wrath[405] but for Conscience sake; and we ought to make supplications and prayers for Kings, and all that are in Authority,[406] that under them we may live a quiet and peaceable life, in all godliness and honesty.

---

402 *Rom. 13 1,2,3,4.*
403 *2 Sam. 23.3. Ps. 82.3,4.*
404 *Luk. 3.14.*
405 *Rom. 13.5,6,7. 1 Pet. 2.17.*
406 *1 Tim. 2.1,2.*

Chapter XXV

Of Marriage

1. Marriage is to be between one Man and one Woman;[407] neither is it lawful for any man to have more than one Wife, nor for any Woman to have more than one Husband at the same time.

2. Marriage was ordained for the mutual help[408] of Husband and Wife,[409] for the increase of Man-kind, with a legitimate issue, and for[410] preventing of uncleanness.

3. It is lawful for[411] all sorts of people to Marry, who are able with judgment to give their consent; yet it is the duty of Christians[412] to marry in the Lord, and therefore such as profess the true Religion, should not Marry with Infidels,[413] or Idolaters; neither should such as are godly be unequally yoked, by marrying with such as are wicked, in their life, or maintain damnable Heresy.

4. Marriage ought not to be within the degrees of consanguinity,[414] or Affinity forbidden in the word; nor can such incestuous Marriage ever be made lawful, by any law of Man or consent of parties,[415] so as those persons may live together as Man and Wife.

---

[407] *Gen. 2.24. Mal. 2 15. Mat. 19.5,6.*
[408] *Gen. 2.18.*
[409] *Gen 1.28.*
[410] *1 Cor. 7 2,9.*
[411] *Heb. 13,4. 1 Tim. 4,3.*
[412] *1 Cor. 7.39.*
[413] *Neh. 13 25,26,27.*
[414] *Levit. 18.*
[415] *Mar. 6.18. 1 Cor. 5.1.*

Chapter XXVI

Of *the* Church

1. The Catholic or universal Church, which (with respect to the internal work of the Spirit, and truth of grace) may be called invisible, consists of the whole[416] number of the Elect, that have been, are, or shall be gathered into one, under Christ the head thereof; and is the spouse, the body, the fullness of him that filleth all in all.

2. All persons throughout the world, professing the faith of the Gospel, and obedience unto God by Christ, according unto it; not destroying their own profession by any Errors averting the foundation, or unholyness of conversation,[417] are and may be called visible Saints;[418] and of such ought all particular Congregations to be constituted.

3. The purest Churches under heaven are subject[419] to mixture, and error; and some have so degenerated as to become[420] no Churches of Christ, but Synagogues of Satan; nevertheless Christ always hath had, and ever shall have a[421] Kingdome in this world, to the end thereof, of such as believe in him, and make profession of his Name.

4. The Lord Jesus Christ is the Head of the Church, in whom by the appointment of the Father,[422] all power for the calling, institution, order, or Government of the Church, is invested in a supreme & sovereign manner, neither can the Pope of Rome in any sense be head thereof, but is[423] that Antichrist, that Man of sin, and Son of perdition, that exalteth himself in the Church against Christ,

---

[416] *Heb. 12.23. Col. 1.18. Eph. 1.10,22.23. & ch. 5.23,27,32.*
[417] *1 Cor. 1 2. Act. 11.26.*
[418] *Rom. 1.7. Eph. 1.20,21,22.*
[419] *1 Cor. 5:1-13. Rev. 2. & ch. 3.*
[420] *Rev. 18.2. 2 Thes. 2.11,12.*
[421] *Mat. 16.18. Ps. 72.17. & Ps. 102.28. Rev. 12.17.*
[422] *Col. 1.18. Mat. 28.18,19.20. Eph. 4.11,12.*
[423] *2 Thes. 2.3-9.*

and all that is called God; whom the Lord shall destroy with the brightness of his coming.[424]

5. In the execution of this power wherewith He is so entrusted, the Lord Jesus calleth out of the World unto himself, through the Ministry of his word, by his Spirit,[425] those that are given unto Him by his Father; that they may walk before Him in all the[426] ways of obedience, which He prescribeth to them in his Word. Those thus called He commands to walk together in particular societies, or[427] Churches, for their mutual edification; and the due performance of that public worship, which He requireth of them in the World.

6. The Members of these Churches are[428] Saints by calling, visibly manifesting and evidencing (in and by their profession and walking) their obedience unto that call of Christ; and do willingly consent to walk together according to the appointment of Christ, giving up themselves, to the Lord & one to another by the will of God,[429] in professed subjection to the Ordinances of the Gospel.

7. To each of these Churches thus gathered, according to his mind, declared in his word, He hath given all that[430] power and authority, which is any way needful, for their carrying on that order in worship, and discipline, which He hath instituted for them to observe; with commands, and rules, for the due and right exerting, and executing of that power.

8. A particular Church gathered, and completely Organized, according to the mind of Christ, consists of Officers, and Members; And the Officers appointed by Christ to be chosen and set apart by the Church (so called and gathered) for the peculiar Administration of Ordinances, and Execution of Power, or Duty, which He entrusts them with, or calls them to, to be continued to the end of the World are[431] Bishops or Elders and Deacons.

---

[424] *2 Thessalonians 2:2-9.*
[425] *Joh 10.16. chap. 12,32.*
[426] *Mat. 28.20.*
[427] *Mat. 18.15-20.*
[428] *Rom. 1.7. 1 Cor. 1.2.*
[429] *Act. 2.41,42. ch. 5.13.14. 2 Cor. 9.13.*
[430] *Mat. 18.17,18. 1 Cor. 5.4,5. with v. 13. 2 Cor. 2.6,7,8.*
[431] *Act. 20:17, with v. 28. Phil. 1.1.*

9. The way appointed by Christ for the Calling of any person, fitted, and gifted by the Holy Spirit, unto the Office of Bishop, or Elder, in a Church, is, that He be chosen thereunto by the common[432] suffrage of the Church itself; and Solemnly set apart by Fasting and Prayer, with imposition of hands of the[433] Eldership of the Church, if there be any before Constituted therein; And of a Deacon[434] that He be chosen by the like suffrage, and set apart by Prayer, and the like Imposition of hands.

10. The work of Pastors being constantly to attend the Service of Christ, in his Churches, in the Ministry of the Word, and Prayer,[435] with watching for their Souls, as they that must give an account to him; it is incumbent on the Churches to whom they Minister, not only to give them all due respect,[436] but also to communicate to them of all their good things according to their ability, so as they may have a comfortable supply, without being themselves[437] entangled in Secular Affairs; and may also be capable of exercising[438] Hospitality toward others; and this is required by the[439] Law of Nature, and by the Express order of our Lord Jesus, who hath ordained that they that preach the Gospel, should live of the Gospel.

11. Although it be incumbent on the Bishops or Pastors of the Churches to be instant in Preaching the Word, by way of Office; yet the work of Preaching the Word, is not so peculiarly confined to them; but that others also[440] gifted, and fitted by the Holy Spirit for it, and approved, and called by the Church, may and ought to perform it.

12. As all Believers are bound to join themselves to particular Churches, when and where they have opportunity so to do; so all that are admitted unto the privileges of a Church, are also[441] under

---

[432] *Act. 14.23*
[433] *1 Tim. 4.14.*
[434] *Act. 6.3.5.6.*
[435] *Act. 6.4. Heb. 13.17.*
[436] *1 Tim. 5.17,18. Gal. 6.6,7.*
[437] *2 Tim. 2.4.*
[438] *1 Tim. 3.2.*
[439] *1 Cor. 9.6.-14.*
[440] *Act. 11.19,20,21. 1 Pet. 4.10.11.*
[441] *1 Thes. 5.14. 2 Thes 3.6.14,15.*

the Censures and Government thereof, according to the Rule of Christ.

13. No Church-members upon any offence taken by them, having performed their Duty required of them towards the person they are offended at, ought to disturb any Church order, or absent themselves from the Assemblies of the Church, or Administration of any Ordinances, upon the account of such offence at any of their fellow-members; but to wait upon Christ,[442] in the further proceeding of the Church.

14. As each Church, and all the Members of it are bound to[443] pray continually, for the good and prosperity of all the Churches of Christ, in all places; and upon all occasions to further it (everyone within the bounds of their places, and callings, in the Exercise of their Gifts and Graces) so the Churches (when planted by the providence of God so as they may enjoy opportunity and advantage for it) ought to hold[444] communion amongst themselves for their peace, increase of love, and mutual edification.

15. In cases of difficulties or differences, either in point of Doctrine, or Administration; wherein either the Churches in general are concerned, or any one Church in their peace, union, and edification; or any member, or members, of any Church are injured, in or by any proceedings in censures not agreeable to truth, and order: it is according to the mind of Christ, that many Churches holding communion together, do by their messengers meet to consider,[445] and give their advice, in or about that matter in difference, to be reported to all the Churches concerned; howbeit these messengers assembled are not entrusted with any Church-power properly so called; or with any jurisdiction over the Churches themselves, to exercise any censures either over any Churches, or Persons: or[446] to impose their determination on the Churches, or Officers.

---

[442] *Mat. 18.15.16,17. Eph. 4 2,3.*
[443] *Eph. 6.18. Ps. 122.6.*
[444] *Rom. 16.1,2. 3 Joh. 8,9,10.*
[445] *Act. 15.2,4,6. & 22,23.25.*
[446] *2 Cor. 1.24. 1 Joh. 4.1.*

Chapter XXVII

Of *the* Communion *of* Saints

1. All Saints that are united to Jesus Christ their Head, by his Spirit, and Faith; although they are not made thereby one person with him, have[447] fellowship in his Graces, sufferings, death, resurrection, and glory; and being united to one another in love, they[448] have communion in each other's gifts, and graces; and are obliged to the performance of such duties, public and private, in an orderly way,[449] as do conduce to their mutual good, both in the inward and outward man.

2. Saints by profession are bound to maintain an holy fellowship and communion in the worship of God, and in performing such other spiritual services,[450] as tend to their mutual edification; as also in relieving each other in[451] outward things according to their several abilities, and necessities; which communion according to the rule of the Gospel, though especially to be exercised by them, in the relations wherein they stand, whether in[452] families, or[453] Churches; yet as God offereth opportunity is to be extended to all the household of faith, even all those who in every place call upon the name of the Lord Jesus; nevertheless their communion one with another as Saints, doth not take away or[454] infringe, the title or propriety, which each man hath in his goods and possessions.

---

[447] *1 Joh. 1.3. Joh. 1.16. Phil. 3 10 Rom. 6.5 6.*
[448] *Eph. 4.15.16. 1 Cor. 12.7. 1 Cor. 3 21,22,23.*
[449] *1 Thes. 5.11.14. Rom. 1.12. 1 Joh. 3.17.18. Gal 6.10.*
[450] *Heb. 10 24,25. with ch. 3.12,13.*
[451] *Acts 11:29,30.*
[452] *Eph. 6.4.*
[453] *1 Cor. 12.14.-27.*
[454] *Act. 5.4. Eph. 4.28.*

Chapter XXVIII

Of Baptism *and the* Lord's Supper

1. Baptism and the Lords Supper are ordinances of positive, and sovereign institution; appointed by the Lord Jesus the only Lawgiver, to be continued in his Church[455] to the end of the world.

2. These holy appointments are to be administered by those only, who are qualified and thereunto called according[456] to the commission of Christ.

---

[455] *Mat. 28 19,20. 1 Cor. 11.26.*
[456] *Mat. 28.19. 1 Cor. 4.1.*

Chapter XXIX

Of Baptism

1. Baptism is an Ordinance of the New Testament, ordained by Jesus Christ, to be unto the party Baptized, a sign of his fellowship with him, in his death, [457] and resurrection; of his being engrafted into him; of[458] remission of sins; and of his[459] giving up unto God through Jesus Christ to live and walk in newness of Life.

2. Those who do actually profess[460] repentance towards God, faith in, and obedience, to our Lord Jesus, are the only proper subjects of this ordinance.

3. The outward element to be used in this ordinance[461] is water, wherein the party is to be baptized, in the name of the Father, and of the Son, and of the Holy Spirit.

4. Immersion, or dipping of the person[462] in water, is necessary to the due administration of this ordinance.

---

[457] *Rom. 6.3,4,5. Col. 2.12. Gal. 3.27.*
[458] *Mar. 1.4. Act. 22.16.*
[459] *Rom, 6.2,4.*
[460] *Mar. 16.16. Act. 8.36,37.*
[461] *Mat 28.19,20. with Act. 8.38.*
[462] *Mat. 3.16. Joh. 3 23.*

Chapter XXX

Of *the* Lord's Supper

1. The Supper of the Lord Jesus, was instituted by Him, the same night wherein He was betrayed, to be observed in his Churches unto the end of the world, for the perpetual remembrance, and showing forth the sacrifice of himself in his death[463] confirmation of the faith of believers in all the benefits thereof, their spiritual nourishment, and growth in him, their further engagement in, and to, all duties which they owe unto Him;[464] and to be a bond and pledge of their communion with Him, and with each other.

2. In this ordinance Christ is not offered up to his Father, nor any real sacrifice made at all, for remission of sin of the quick or dead; but only a memorial of that[465] one offering up of himself, by himself, upon the cross, once for all; and a spiritual oblation of all[466] possible praise unto God for the same; so that the Popish sacrifice of the Mass (as they call it) is most abominable, injurious to Christ's own only sacrifice, the alone propitiation for all the sins of the Elect.

3. The Lord Jesus hath in this Ordinance, appointed his Ministers to Pray, and bless the Elements of Bread and Wine, and thereby to set them apart from a common to an holy use, and to take and break the Bread; to take the Cup,[467] and (they communicating also themselves) to give both to the Communicants.

4. The denial of the Cup to the people, worshiping the Elements, the lifting them up, or carrying them about for adoration, and reserving them for any pretended religious use,[468] are all contrary to the nature of this Ordinance, and to the institution of Christ.

---

463 *1 Cor. 11.23,24.25,26.*
464 *1 Cor. 10.16,17.21.*
465 *Heb. 9.25,26.28.*
466 *1 Cor. 11.24. Mat. 26.26,27.*
467 *1 Cor. 11.23,24,25,26, etc.*
468 *Mat 26.26,27,28. Mat. 15.9. Exod. 20.4,5.*

5. The outward Elements in this Ordinance, duly set apart to the uses ordained by Christ, have such relation to Him crucified, as that truly, although in terms used figuratively, they are sometimes called by the name of the things they represent, to wit the[469] body and Blood of Christ; albeit in substance, and nature, they still remain truly, and only[470] Bread, and Wine, as they were before.

6. That doctrine which maintains a change of the substance of Bread and Wine, into the substance of Christ's body and blood (commonly called Transubstantiation) by consecration of a Priest, or by any other way, is repugnant not to Scripture[471] alone, but even to common sense and reason; overthroweth the[472] nature of the ordinance, and hath been and is the cause of manifold superstitions, yea, of gross Idolatries.

7. Worthy receivers, outwardly partaking of the visible Elements in this Ordinance, do then also inwardly by faith, really and indeed, yet not carnally, and corporally, but spiritually receive, and feed upon Christ crucified[473] & all the benefits of his death: the Body and Blood of Christ, being then not corporally, or carnally, but spiritually present to the faith of Believers, in that Ordinance, as the Elements themselves are to their outward senses.

8. All ignorant and ungodly persons, as they are unfit to enjoy communion[474] with Christ; so are they unworthy of the Lords Table; and cannot without great sin against him, while they remain such, partake of these holy mysteries,[475] or be admitted thereunto: yea whosoever shall receive unworthily are guilty of the Body and Blood of the Lord, eating and drinking judgment to themselves.

---

[469] *1 Cor. 11.27.*
[470] *1 Cor. 11.26. & v. 28.*
[471] *Act. 3.21. Luk. 24.6.*
[472] *1 Cor. 11.24,25.*
[473] *1 Cor. 10.16. ch. 11.23-26.*
[474] *2 Cor: 6,14,15.*
[475] *1 Cor. 11.29. Mat. 7.6.*

Chapter XXXI

Of *the* State *of* Man *after* Death
and of the Resurrection *of the* Dead

1. The Bodies of Men after Death return to dust,[476] and see corruption; but their Souls (which neither die nor sleep) having an immortal subsistence, immediately[477] return to God who gave them: the Souls of the Righteous being then made perfect in holiness, are received into paradise where they are with Christ, and behold the face of God, in light[478] and glory; waiting for the full Redemption of their Bodies; and the souls of the wicked, are cast into hell; where they remain in torment and utter darkness, reserved to[479] the judgment of the great day; besides these two places for Souls separated from their bodies, the Scripture acknowledgeth none.

2. At the last day such of the Saints as are found alive shall not sleep but be[480] changed; and all the dead shall be raised up with the self same bodies, and[481] none other; although with different[482] qualities, which shall be united again to their Souls forever.

3. The bodies of the unjust shall by the power of Christ, be raised to dishonor; the bodies of the just by his spirit unto honor,[483] and be made conformable to his own glorious Body.

---

[476] *Gen. 3.19. Act. 13.36.*
[477] *Eccles. 12.7.*
[478] *Luk. 23.43. 2 Cor. 5.1,6,8. Phil. 1.23. Heb. 12.23.*
[479] *Jud. 6,7. 1 Pet. 3.19. Luk. 16.23,24.*
[480] *1 Cor. 15: 51,52. 1 Thes. 4.17.*
[481] *Job 19.26,27.*
[482] *1 Cor. 15.42,43.*
[483] *Act. 24.15. Joh. 5.28,29. Phil. 3.21.*

Chapter XXXII

Of *the* Last Judgment

1. God hath appointed a Day wherein He will judge the world in Righteousness, by[484] Jesus Christ; to whom all power and judgment is given of the Father; in which Day not only the[485] Apostate Angels shall be judged; but likewise all persons that have lived upon the Earth, shall appear before the Tribunal of Christ;[486] to give an account of their Thoughts, Words, and Deeds, and to receive according to what they have done in the body, whether good or evil.

2. The end of Gods appointing this Day, is for the manifestation of the glory of his Mercy, in the Eternal Salvation of the Elect;[487] and of his Justice in the Eternal damnation of the Reprobate, who are wicked and disobedient; for then shall the Righteous go into Everlasting Life, and receive that fullness of Joy, and Glory, with everlasting reward, in the presence[488] of the Lord: but the wicked who know not God, and obey not the Gospel of Jesus Christ, shall be cast into Eternal torments, and[489] punished with everlasting destruction, from the presence of the Lord, and from the glory of his power.

3. As Christ would have us to be certainly persuaded that there shall be a Day of judgment, both[490] to deter all men from sin, and for the greater[491] consolation of the godly, in their adversity; so will He have that day unknown to Men, that they may shake off all carnal security, and be always watchful, because they know not at what

---

[484] *Act. 17.31. Joh. 5.22,27.*

[485] *1 Cor. 6.3. Jud. 6.*

[486] *2 Cor. 5.10. Eccles. 12.14. Mat. 12.36. Rom. 14.10,12. Mat. 25.32. etc.*

[487] *Rom. 9.22,23.*

[488] *Mat. 25.21,34. 2 Tim. 4.8.*

[489] *Mat. 25.46. Mar. 9.48. 2 Thes. 1.7,8,9,10.*

[490] *2 Cor. 5.10,11.*

[491] *2 Thes. 1.5,6,7.*

hour, the[492] Lord will come; and may ever be prepared to say,[493] Come Lord Jesus, Come quickly, Amen.

CPSIA information can be obtained
at www.ICGtesting.com
Printed in the USA
LVHW101956091121
702882LV00002B/57

9 781603 868761